Cover by Designer Extraordinaire Annme Spiby!

We may be reached electronically at
authorjimhenry@gmail.com

The World According to Crash Politics, Money & Stuff
is lovingly dedicated to my parents, Richard & Ruth Henry.
Love you folks!

Thank You So Much for Picking Up
The World According to Crash – Politics, Money & Stuff!
If you enjoy it, we would be honored with a review. If you
do not enjoy it, we hope something heavy drops on top of
you so you may forget you didn't like it before writing a
review!

About This Book

In the event that you have not picked up a copy of the earlier books in this series, including **The World According to Crash – Miscellaneous Stuff & Stuff!** and **The World According to Crash Even More Stuff!** I thought I should explain about this book.

Many of the articles included in this book are pieces that I have written previously, along the theme of Politics, Money & Stuff. So if some of the material sounds sort of, well, dated, that would explain it. This is particularly applicable to the material pertaining to President Obama's first election in 2008. Funny thing is that some of the lessons from that election are still highly relevant as candidates start lining up to replace him in 2016.

Of course, there are newer pieces too, some of which I hope will make you chuckle, and some of which will make you think while you chuckle.

And so, without further ado, let me thank you for picking up this copy of **The World According to Crash – Politics, Money & Stuff!**

Table of Contents

The Politics of Poverty

I was just listening to the radio while waiting for my son's bus to come and pick him up for another day at school. There was a story about a woman who lives in Miami who was desperate. She did not have a job, and she did not have money to buy groceries for her children. So in her desperate state, she made what must have been the difficult decision to steal the food she needed to feed her children.

As fate would have it, she was caught, but this turned out to be the best thing that could have happened to her.

Getting arrested being the best thing? No, that would not have been a positive outcome, because it would not have solved a thing. Had the mother been arrested, odds are that she would have lost her children. I do not know this for a fact, but my guess is that she was a single mom, and who knows where the dad or dads were. She did what she felt she had to do to feed her children.

Well, the self-righteous say there's always food stamps and food pantries, right? Sure, but look a little further into this book and see how easy it is to get food stamps in the state of Florida. Make that, see how next-to-impossible it is to overcome the Department of Children and Families' unique brand of incompetence.

Let me tell you another story.

There was a middle-aged woman I know who lived in Lakeland, Florida. She was disabled, living on SSDI, and barely making ends meet.

It came time for this woman to go through the periodic six month inquisition and torture experience known as re-certification. This, true believers, is when DCF really shows off how completely incompetent the agency is. I happen to know that this woman's complete monthly income was just shy of $600. Her rent was $400. Her electric bill usually ran about $150, which left her with about $50 left over for all the incidentals she incurred on a monthly basis. By no one's standards is this woman well-off.

Somehow, though, when DCF looked at her income, they saw her making much more money than she actually did. How? In their estimation, her husband's income should be combined with her income. Problem was that she and her husband, though not legally divorced, had been separated for several years, maintaining separate residences. He was raising three of their children, and she had one who was legally considered his, because they were still married, but who was biologically another man's child, and who came into the world after they had separated.

As a result of this screw up, DCF slashed her food stamps completely. She did not have a car, so her only means of getting to a food pantry was by bus, but getting around by bus in her city was very difficult, especially when toting around a hyper-active two year-old boy.

When her cupboards became more bare, this woman did not choose to steal as the woman from Miami did. Instead, she made the difficult decision to go grocery shopping, using the money she normally would have paid for rent, so she could feed her child.

The end of her story is not as pleasant as the woman from Miami. She did manage to convince DCF that she and her husband were no longer living together, and they responded by giving her the food stamps they never should have taken in the first place. But food stamps do not pay the rent, and eventually the park manager in her mobile home park moved to evict her. As I write this story, she is trying to figure out how to get her stuff out of the trailer before the park manager removes it and leaves it on the side of the road. Odds are she won't get it done.

But don't worry about her. Though her future ex-husband does not want to revisit the traumatic existence that led to their separation three years ago, he is not about to let the mother of his children languish in a homeless shelter, because it matters little to him that her baby is not really his. A homeless shelter is no place to live for anyone, but definitely not for a child. So he has agreed, warily, to let her and her child move in with him until he can scrape up the money necessary to help her move into another dumpy trailer closer to him and her children living with him.

Back to the woman from Miami. Her situation does have a happy ending, so far as I can see. Turns out that the police officer who came to the store to arrest her had a conscience, and when she heard exactly why the woman was forced to steal to support her children, the officer decided that arresting her would serve no purpose, because it would not solve the problem.

Instead, using her own funds, the police officer spent $100 out of her own pocket to buy groceries for the woman and her children.

The DJ on the radio station said that when the police officer brought the groceries to the woman's home, it was like Christmas morning for those kids, and no doubt it warmed her heart to see how happy the children were to have food.

The story gets better, though. When the word got out about what the police officer had done, and the plight of the woman, the DJ on WKTK-FM reported that many other people donated more than $700 for the woman to buy groceries for her children. What's more, a store owner heard about her situation, called her in for an interview, and hired her on the spot, so now she has a job to help support her children.

That may not solve all her problems, though. I recently stopped in a CVS store in Bushnell, Florida and bought a gallon of milk to bring home. For some reason, the clerk whom I paid for the milk felt compelled to tell me that although she obviously was working, she had been fighting with DCF to get extra help to make ends meet. She told me that even if she were to be approved for TANF (Temporary Assistance for Needy Families) from the state of Florida (which she couldn't, because basically the only people who get TANF here are those who have absolutely no income whatsoever) she would actually have to pay the money back to the state of Florida, by way of payroll deductions.

Imagine that! A person goes from being so broke that she qualifies for TANF in Florida, finally gets a minimum wage job working in retail, and the state of Florida says, "Congratulations on your new job! We'll just take back a piece of that because we gave you a whopping $306 a month when you could not support your family."

Now, the Ultra-Conservative Neo-Nazi Fascist Pigs out there are probably saying, "Good! No hand-outs in Florida! I got a job, I worked hard to support my family, why can't they?"

Programs like SNAP (food stamps) and TANF should be a safety net to prevent parents from having to resort to stealing from the local Wally World to feed their children. I would not suggest that the poor should be subsidized to such a degree that they can live a middle-class lifestyle, but the idea that TANF recipients should have to pay back the paltry little sum the state of Florida allows them to receive is laughable.

Jumping down from my soap box for now.....

A Third of SSDI Recipients Fraudulent? Really?

Tom Ufert is a best-selling author with several titles to his credit. I first got to know Tom after stumbling across his book *Adversity Builds Character: An Inspirational True Life Story of Disability, Addiction, and Acceptance.* As I was collecting information to include in this book, I read a highly articulate (no surprise there) letter Tom sent to Senator Tom Coburn, after the Republican legislator made disparaging remarks about people on Social Security Disability, while appearing on the Cable News Network.

After reading his letter, I wrote to Tom Ufert and asked his permission to include his thoughtful words in this book, which he graciously gave me permission. Without further ado, here is Tom Ufert's letter to Sen. Coburn:

Dear Senator Coburn,

After seeing your appearance on CNN's New Day program this morning I was outraged by your comments regarding the accusation that 1/3 of those receiving disability payments/ services from Social Security were fraudulent. As a 21 year recipient of these services due to three different life altering disabilities (MS, HIV, and an incomplete spinal fracture C5/C6), I can assure you that your accusation doesn't fit my conditions.

Nonetheless, this inflammatory public discourse however, directly affects public perceptions of the disabled. While I totally concur with efforts to seek out and prosecute SS fraud, your insinuations adversely affect those of us that struggle daily to survive on our rightly earned benefits. After numerous efforts to work and failing due to the increased fatigue that exacerbated my debilitating health issues, my doctor decided that my overall health could not permit continued employment. As a doctor you must be acutely aware that not all disabilities are visually detectable.

I would suggest that you should put your Hippocratic oath before your Right-wing agenda and take more caution when seeking to broadly categorize the disabled in the public arena. Your outrageous comments greatly offended me and unfairly stereotyped SS Disability recipients. Only a public apology from you for this disgraceful language is acceptable. Please continue your efforts to root out SS fraud, but take care in such derogatory broad classifications...I guarantee you, come election day, you may severely regret such public accusations.

Most Respectfully yours,
Tom Ufert

This letter resonated with me for a variety of reasons. Probably the biggest reason is because members of my own family, including my oldest son and his mother, are considered disabled. The process we endured to prove the disability for both of them was lengthy. They had to be evaluated by their doctors, by independent doctors, there were hearings involved. Although both were ultimately approved for benefits, the process it took to get there was long and arduous. For a licensed medical doctor and public official like Tom Coburn to say that fully one-third of the people receiving benefits are doing so fraudulently is shocking.

Even if Coburn is correct in his assessment, (I do not believe that to be the case) would this not be an indictment of the evaluation system as much as it is reflective of the people who receive benefits without deserving it?

This is one of the problems I have with many Republicans. My suspicion is that Senator Coburn would love to point to this problem as proof that we should throw out the baby with the bathwater. The problem is, even with Senator Coburn's estimates, two-thirds of those receiving benefits actually deserve them, so it would seem to be draconian to throw out the whole system, rather than trying to fix what is wrong with it.

Where Are Florida's Priorities?

Take a look at the screenshot I took on October 9, 2013 of the state of Florida's website to help people find health insurance. Perhaps by the time you read this, the state will have updated the page so it can be helpful to individuals and employees. Here is the URL: https://www.floridahealthchoices.com/ .

Don't you think it is illustrative that nine days after people should have been able to begin searching for healthcare under the Affordable Care Act (AKA

Obamacare), the state of Florida only has information that is valuable for employers and agents seeking insurance for clients, but not for employees, individuals or families?

Unemployment Delayed Because You Were Honest

I just received a phone call - on a Saturday no less! - from a supervisor at the unemployment office. He was returning my call from earlier in the week, trying to respond to why I was not receiving payment for two weeks of unemployment claims back in December. Problem is, as I noted yesterday, the matter was finally resolved by the adjudicator yesterday, and the money finally arrived in my checkbook this morning. So basically this supervisor finally got around to calling me AFTER the problem was resolved (in my favor, no less!)

As long as I had him on the phone, though, I decided to pick his brain a bit. It turns out that the reason why this problem happened, though, is because I answered the questions in filing the claim honestly.

Seriously.

It turns out that the issue arose because I put into the system that I had a return date for work. In the old days, before the new computer system, this was a good thing to report, because reporting that I had a firm call back date meant that I would not have to do a job search, since I was only in between assignments as opposed to being unemployed for the foreseeable future.

Now, though, with the new system they have, even if I am off work only for a week or two, I still have to report at least five employer contacts for each week I claim, even if it is to my past (and future) employer all five times! Plus, by indicating that I have a firm call-back date, the computer system flags that claim and forces it to an adjudicator, and makes me jump through all kinds of hoops to prove that I am not presently working, or was not during the weeks claimed.

So I said to this supervisor, Rodney, that it sounds like I should not indicate that I have a call back date, if that is what happens when you do. Incredulously, he said that if I do have a firm call back date, I must report it, so they can be sure they are not paying unemployment benefits when I am back to work.

I said to the guy that I am a straight shooter. If I am not working, I file a claim. If I am working, I don't. And if I am working just a little, I will report the earnings accurately, and if I am entitled to benefits I will gladly take them. If not, I will not file.

I then told him that back in mid-December, I had a week in between classes from one of my employers, and I was teaching just one class for the other employer. I told him that for that week I reported the income for the employer for whom I was still teaching, and reported no income for the other employer, because that was the truth.

In Florida, they have us file two weeks at a time. By the second week, I was teaching for both schools, and my income rose above the level I would be allowed to collect, and I reported all those earnings, so I collected just one week for a partial claim, and I had no trouble collecting that week. Contrast that with what happened when I was totally unemployed for the following two weeks during the holidays, can anyone see a reason why I should not tell them I have a firm call back date the next time I have to file a claim? I can't!

Serve.....Are You Serious?

A while ago, back when I was not working so hard that I have no life outside of work, I was playing Bubble Safari a lot on Facebook. One time they had a promotion that if I signed up for a Serve prepaid debit card, I would get a bunch of coins to use in Bubble Safari. So I signed up for it, but then the card never came.

For the most part, I forgot about it but every month I receive an email from the Serve card talking about account activity for an account that I never received. So just now, upon seeing the latest such email, I decided to call them and tell them that I had never received a card. I mentioned to the customer service flunky with a strong foreign accent that I had even moved since asking for this card.

She was able to locate my account, and was willing to send me a card, but in order to update my address, I was going to have to go to their website, print out a form and fax it to them to change my address.

Really?

If this were a real credit card, you can bet your butt, my butt, my dog Punker's butt, or anyone's butt that they would want to make for damned sure they knew where I was living, and they would not require me to jump through hoops like this.

"How about this," I said. "I do not have a fax machine, and my printer is out of ink, so it is much more work than I care to do to print out this form, fill it out and fax it back to you. So why don't we just close this account?"

"Well, if you do not want to fax it to us, you could always print it out and mail it to us."

"Well, again, my printer is out of ink, and it is not worth it to me to drive to the library to print out this form, and then stick it into an envelope and waste one of my stamps to mail it back to you, so why don't we just close the account?"

"OK, I can do that for you sir. Let me just tell you that I will close the account today, but if you wish to reactivate the card within 30 days, we will be able to reactivate it, but after 31 days, the account will be closed forever."

"Really? Do you promise?"

I'm betting that I get another Serve Monthly Statement email next month.

We are Stuck with the Second Amendment

You know, I'm going to stick my neck out here because it is the right thing to do. I am sure there will be all kinds of people attacking me for what I am about to report, because I know many Americans hold the right to bear arms more dearly than the right of a free press or the right to practice religion as we wish.

Today someone shot a bullet into a window at the Obama campaign office in Denver, Colorado. There were people inside the building when the terrorist shot at their store front. Thankfully no one was injured, but that is of little consequence, because I firmly believe the shooter intended to hurt or kill someone who is merely working for the candidate for president of his or her choosing.

Then there is the case of a Pakistani activist named Malala who has been speaking out forcefully and articulately for the Pakistani government to allow females to go to school. For this "offense" the Taliban in Pakistan shot her, intending to end her life. Fortunately, she lives, at least for now, though the next 48 hours will be incredibly important.

Now, some might say that I cannot blame what happened to Malala on the second amendment, because it happened in a foreign country. Fair enough. How about Gabby Giffords, the former Congresswoman who was shot by a gun-toting would-be assassin? Gun laws did not protect Gabby. Gun laws did not prevent the gunman who shot at the Obama headquarters from shooting at it. And gun laws did not protect Malala who was exercising her God-given right to speak (a right the Pakistani government does not apparently recognize yet).

The problem is the second amendment. In a nation that has the strongest military in the world, we are protected. We do not need to bear arms to protect ourselves. The primary purpose of guns is to kill, and far too often barbaric humans use guns to kill each other.

I don't know diddly about managing my money!

It's true! So why, then, would I be writing on this subject? Well, for starters because it was one of my goals for 2009 to write a article on each and every hubmob weekly topic, so even though I am now, always have been, and probably always will be, a complete idiot when it comes to finances, I am going to give this a go. Plus, I actually know a fair amount about such subjects, it's just that I have a hard time taking my own advice when it comes to money management.

The Best Way to Make Money is the Old-Fashioned Way: Work!

I know the ultra-conservative Neo-Nazi fascist pigs out there would love to believe that every family on welfare is secretly living the high life on the public dole, but let me tell you, nothing could be further from the truth. Welfare, or Transitional Aid for Families in Need (I think that's what TANF means), is barely a subsistence level existence in the most liberal of states, and is hardly worth the effort of applying in the more conservative states in America. And the notion that having more babies is going to help is laughable. Sure, you'll see an increase in your monthly TANF check, but it will not come close to matching the increased expenditures that new member of the family for whom you are now responsible will incur.

So the bottom line is that if you want security for your family, getting a job is the biggest step you can take toward financial security. Of course, that's easier said than done, in today's economy. That does not give you permission to sit on your butt and wait for things to get better. Instead, you should be starting your job search immediately! Start networking! Go to job fairs! You never know which contact you make today that may result in an opportunity down the line.

I'll give you an example. I am presently teaching for the University of Phoenix Online and Ashford University Online. I love online teaching because you can't beat the commute, I get to work at home and be there when my kids get off the school bus, and as long as I have a computer with an Internet connection, I'm golden. I got my foot in the door when the University of Phoenix needed people with communications and journalism background to teach one of their introductory classes, called "Contemporary Business Communications." I believe that just about every new student to enroll in Axia College of the University of Phoenix must take this class, whether they want to or not. So as long as I do the job that is expected of me, I've got job security. Online education is booming, for the same reasons why I love teaching online.

A Poor Economy Is A Great Time To Pursue A Degree

The reason why people like me are getting work for these online programs is because many people who are either unemployed, underemployed, or afraid they'll become either of the above, decide that the time is now to go back to school and get their degree. But they don't want to uproot their family, and if they are employed, they don't want to quit their job just to pursue a degree. So the solution is to take classes from the comfort of your own home, online. You could also take classes at a local community college, as most of them tend to be pretty affordable. A degree will make you that much more marketable when the economy improves (and it will, it always does, even after the Great Depression).

The Next Topic – Taxes

The worst way to manage your money is to let the government take extra money out of your paycheck every week or two, depending upon how often you get paid. Sure, I'm the first to admit that a near sexual thrill overcomes me when I get my tax return back, but in reality what has happened is that you've let the government take your money, use it to pay for $200 toilet seats, and then give it back to you a year later, without interest. Instead, the best way to manage your money is to have just enough money withheld from your check so you can break even, or perhaps get a small tax return. In that way, you'll be keeping more money in your pocket on a paycheck-by-paycheck basis, which you can use to buy your own $200 toilet seat, if that's what you want to do. The bottom line (no pun intended) is that it's always better in a bad economy to have access to every dime you have at your disposal.

While we're talking about taxes, I've got to say a word about the Earned Income Credit. When I get my taxes back, just about all of the return (which I actually mailed out today) will be in the form of the Earned Income Credit. The amount of your credit depends upon how much or how little earned income you actually had, your family size, etc. It's a great way to really blow up that return, but you have to be careful to be honest about your income. If our friendly auditors at the IRS find that you have exaggerated your income in order to qualify for a higher earned income credit, there can be serious consequences, not the least of which is that they can ban you from taking the credit in future years (I think it's two years, but I could be wrong there). The important thing, as I said before, is to be brutally honest, and in the end, you'll have some gravy to put on your mashed potatoes.

This is HUGE! Check Your Credit Annually!

A couple years ago, I started getting into the habit, just after New Year's, to request copies of my credit report from all three of the major credit reporting agencies. These companies - TransUnion, Experian and Equifax - make their money by selling reports on you to potential employers, landlords, bank officers, etc. The quality of their report, therefore, is inextricably linked to how much value any of those potential clients place on the information. In that regard, each of those companies actually want people to dispute information contained in their credit report if in fact it is erroneous. Depending upon whom you talk to, up to 80 percent of all credit reports contain at least one error.

It is against the law to try to mislead the credit bureaus to remove items from your credit report when it is actually accurate. Fortunately, though, they give you options you can choose from, including one where you can stipulate that you have no knowledge of a particular debt. Such a claim is very nearly impossible to refute, because it's impossible to know what a person can or can not remember. Therefore, when you go through your personal credit report, paying particular attention to the negative items listed, if you have any doubt about whether a particular debt is actually yours, it is in your interest to dispute it. In an initial dispute, the less you say the better. The credit bureaus then have 30 days from the day you submitted your dispute, to contact the creditors and verify the information. If they do verify the information, sometimes the items are updated, to reflect interest that has accrued, or perhaps to reflect payments you may have made to reduce the debt.

If a creditor can not provide documentation within 30 days that you owe this money, by law the item must be removed from your credit report.

The down side of this approach, challenging everything under the Sun, is that once an item has been verified, if you challenge the debt again, particularly too soon, the credit bureau can legally refuse to verify your debt, labeling it "frivolous," since they just jumped through the hoops to prove it was your debt.

Sometimes, however, it is appropriate to contact the creditor directly. I'll give you an example that showed up on my credit report when I pulled them for 2009. According to the TransUnion report, I had a collections debt for over $300 to Maine Medical Center. I checked with Maine Medical Center to find out when this debt was incurred, and they said it was February of 2007. The problem was that in February of 2007, I had full health insurance. So I contacted my insurer and verified that my insurance was, in fact, in force on the date of service. Then I called back Maine Medical Center and informed them that they should have been paid by my insurance company, and added that this negative item on my credit report was affecting my ability to get affordable credit today.

In the end, Maine Medical Center agreed to drop the debt, as it was their error in billing that resulted in not being paid for the service, and they notified their collections agency that the matter had been resolved. All-in-all, I spent about a half-hour making phone calls, and I got that item permanently removed from my credit report.

You can also write letters to creditors and collections agencies, asking them to verify a debt. I have one item on my credit report claiming that I once bounced a check to some company in Seattle for some pictures. I know, based upon the date this check was allegedly written by me, that I did not even have a checking account at that time. So this is one that I am sending a certified letter to, asking them to verify the debt. I'm also asking them to provide me with a copy of the original check, so I can compare the signature on the check against the signature on my driver's license. I fully expect to find that this check was written by someone else with a similar name as mine, and ended up in my credit report.

Of course, the best way to improve your credit is to pay your bills. Even if you have accounts that have been charged off, you can pay off the debt and see your credit worthiness increase. Sometimes you can negotiate with a creditor or collections agency, and reach a deal whereby if you pay down the debt, meeting payment due dates, at the end of the process not only will the negative item be removed from your credit report, but you can also ask the creditor to agree to report it as a positive account. In an economy like we have today, creditors will be much more likely to make concessions like that as long as it results in their company getting money they had long since given up hope on collecting.

One last point about credit - for most negative items on your report, the longest they can remain on your report is seven years. Bankruptcies can stay on longer, up to 10 years, and public judgments by courts can stay on significantly longer (I believe 20 years, but don't quote me on that). So if you check your credit report and see that there is a collections account on your record that is more than seven years old, you should immediately write to the credit bureau and remind them that the item must be removed from your credit report.

UPDATE!

I just received the results back from my challenges to accounts that appeared in one of my credit reports, and found that 10 items I disputed could not be verified. And in this case, it was not because the creditors simply ran out of time. They still had three days left before the items would have been dropped due to the 30 day requirement. So it pays to challenge items you believe to be inaccurate. Just because an item is on your credit report does not mean that you actually owe the money. Credit reports are generated by creditors and collections agencies that are run by human beings. Human beings are prone to making mistakes, and in this case, I would have been doing a disservice to myself by simply accepting the accuracy of these items.

Last, but certainly not least, we have investing!

There's always a safe place to put money you want to invest, but the key is to know where to put it, depending upon the condition of the economy. With the way the stock market has been going up and down like a manic depressant patient, now would not be the time to jump into the stock market. Real estate, too, is not a great option for the short-term because property values are down in most places. On the other hand, if you are looking for a bargain, and intend to keep the property for a while, this is a great time to buy. I contacted a realtor in Florida recently and found that this realtor alone has HUNDREDS of foreclosed, bank-owned properties, many of which can be had for less than the debt that was originally owed.

The key in this case is to have good enough credit in order to qualify for a mortgage, assuming you don't have cash on hand to buy the property outright. That said, there are plenty of properties in the greater Orlando area that you could buy for cash for what would normally be considered a healthy down payment. The key, as I've heard it before, is to try to qualify for the best mortgage you can, with the smallest down payment you can get away with, as long as you can save the money for a rainy day, such as when you may lose your job and need a safety net.

You also have the option of going with a mutual fund, spreading around the types of companies you invest in. I used to have a mutual fund that was split up four ways - 25 percent each for: aggressively managed, conservatively managed, utilities and common stock. By diversifying your portfolio, when the market drops, you've got a fighting chance to weather the storm on Wall Street.

So just remember, folks, that I am by no means an expert on money management, and anything I've said here could very well be worth less than, say, cow patties, and I strongly encourage anyone who reads this to check my facts with people who are not financial idiots and actually know what they're talking about.....of course, George W. Bush has an MBA, and he obviously didn't have a clue on the economy, so who's to say who is an expert these days?

Florida ESE Anything But Exceptional

There is something bugging me, and it has been bugging me for some time. I do not know the answer, and the fact that I may never know the whole answer is probably what is bugging me the most.

My son, whom I affectionately call Boy Wonder, goes to an "Exceptional Student Education" school. His bus comes to pick him up at about 7:15 each morning, and he arrives at the school at about 7:30. They can eat breakfast in the classroom, and academic work begins at 8 a.m. His day ends at 1:30, and he rolls off the school bus on the way home somewhere between 2:00 and 2:15 p.m. Effectively, his learning day is done after five and a half hours.

Contrast that with what my other children have in their mainstream school. They, too, can arrive at 7:30, eat breakfast and be in their classrooms by 8 a.m. Their day, however, goes until 3 p.m., or seven hours of instructional time. On top of that, they offer tutoring to students at the mainstream school who have to take and pass the FCAT Test.

For the first time, this morning, Boy Wonder

36

expressed concern about the FCAT Tests he had to take. Why? Because he says if he does not pass them, he will stay in eighth grade, but he wants to move up to the high school. I know, from my Peanut's experience in third grade last year, that the third grade tests are high stakes, because if she had not passed the tests, she would not have moved up to the fourth grade. I do not know about the eighth grade tests and whether they are high stakes or not, but if someone planted that idea in Boy Wonder's head, there is a good chance that it is true. Regardless, no one ever offered after school tutoring to Boy Wonder to help his chances of passing the test and moving up to the ninth grade.

Here's the real kicker. Fourth grade is not a high stakes testing year for the students. Peanut will move up to fifth grade regardless of how the FCAT scores fall out, as long as her classroom grades remain strong. Despite that, they offered after school tutoring two days a week all year until the FCAT testing started. It looks to me that the purpose of the tutoring is not so much about giving the kids the extra push they need to move up to the next grade level as it is about increasing the school's overall performance on FCAT at all grade levels.

Here's the part that really bugs me. Why is Countywide ESE not as important academically to the Polk County School Department? If they were interested in the academic advancement of their most challenged students, they would not be releasing them from school an hour and a half earlier than mainstream students EVERY SINGLE DAY.

If they were interested in the academic advancement of their most challenged students, they would offer the same after school tutoring opportunities to give them perhaps the leg up they need to move to the next grade level.

The really big question I have is: Why are they not interested in the academic advancement of their mot challenged students? That is the question that bugs me the most, and the one that I doubt will ever be answered.

This is an opportunity to be proactive, and the Polk County School Department is missing the boat. Let's call it the way it is. These students at Countywide ESE are there largely because of behavioral issues. To be sure, most or all of them have academic challenges as well, but they would not be at Countywide if they did not have behavioral problems. These are the kinds of people who, if they have not already done so, are likely to commit crimes that will land them in prison or in juvenile detention one of these days. I live in fear of that every day with Boy Wonder, because I know what he is capable of doing.

Education is the antidote to crime. A well-educated child is much less likely to commit crimes because on a cognitive level that child will know that there are consequences for bad behavior, and those consequences are often severe. Boy Wonder learned that lesson when his mother and I sent him to live in the University Behavioral Center in Orlando for a year, giving him intensive treatment he desperately needed (and many days I think he still needs!) Sadly, I am sure many of the students whom Polk County schools apparently consider throw-aways who will not get a wake-up call in a behavioral hospital. Their wake-up call is likely to be going to juvenile detention or possibly adult prison, and it does not have to be that way.

It seems to me that society in general would benefit greatly from a change in philosophy about how to educate the so-called "exceptional students."

How to Stretch your Dollar When Times are Tough

First the question must be asked, are you presently making enough money to pay your bills and keep food on the table with even a small amount of money left over? If the answer is yes, then you can proceed. My philosophy is that there are basic levels of need that must be met, and sadly there are many people out there who are not meeting their basic needs (through no fault of their own). It would be irresponsible under those circumstances to be socking away money for a rainy day while the family's needs aren't being met. One strategy I've followed, when I've had spare cash, is to treat my savings account like a bill that must be paid. So when I sit down to pay out the electric bill, the rent, the water bill, etc., I also have my savings bill. By doing that, I get into the habit of saving money, which will come in handy someday when the transmission dies, or some other major catastrophe.

Another way to free up cash is to set aside your ego. This has proven to be extremely beneficial to my family. A while ago, I started looking around and found several different food pantries in our vicinity, each with a different set of rules. The Salvation Army lets us come in once a month. So does another food pantry serving citizens from my hometown only. Then there's the one the next town over that will serve anyone in the area, and they let us go there once a week!

In time, we've been able to save a lot of money on groceries by finding free sources of food. Please note that I am not suggesting that the well-off do this. Food pantries are there for folks who really need the food, not just those who are too cheap to pay for it. In my family's case, we're by no means the poorest of the poor, but we do fall below the poverty level, mostly because we have a large family. We still buy some groceries at the supermarket, but a lot of our food comes from food pantries.

A while ago I knew a guy who drove a VW Rabbit diesel. The key here is diesel, because this guy found this handy dandy little device called Mr. Grease, which can be attached to a car running on diesel and allow that car to run on filtered fat from fryolators. This guy didn't have to pay a dime for gas, because all the fast food places were more

41

than happy to donate their used fryolator grease, which at the time they were having to pay to dispose of. Nowadays I suspect a lot of the major chains have gotten wise to this and have started offering their waste product as a commodity to increase their bottom line. Still, I'll bet there are small mom and pop type places that have neither the volume nor the time to seek out such deals, and I'll bet my friend is still driving that VW Rabbit on fryolator grease.

These are just a few of the ways I can think of to stretch your dollar in these difficult economic times. The key is that after you've cut your expenses, and are actually living within your means, that you do take the next step and put that money away somewhere. Depending upon the dynamics of your family, it may be best to put it someplace easily accessible, so it's there for you when you have an emergency. Some families are not that disciplined, and it may be wiser to put the money into a reasonably accessible source, like a six-month CD, which you can later roll over if the circumstances are appropriate.

Here's the Rope Boys

If You Give Them Enough Rope....They WILL Hang Themselves!

I have often contended that if Republicans were smart, they would be Democrats. Another one of my favorite disparaging remarks about the political right is that, like all stupid people, if you give them enough rope they will, in fact, hang themselves!

There were two things in the news that made me shake my head and wonder what planet the Republican leaders live on. The first, and admittedly the one that inspired me to write this article, came courtesy of an early Christmas gift from Senator John Kyl of the great state of Arizona.

Senator Kyl was speaking on a bill before Congress that would provide $8 billion to help fund healthcare costs of the first responders who risked their lives in the World Trade Center, following the 2001 September 11 attack.

Time was, when there was a good ol' boy from Texas in the White House, you could not find a Republican in either house of congress who would not do back flips to do something to help those great American Patriots who were on the front line of the War on Terror before it was even known as the War on Terror.

Now, when we have thousands of first responders who have become ill because of carcinogens to which they were exposed while sifting through the rubble at Ground Zero trying to find survivors of the greatest terrorist attack on American soil in the history of history, we have the likes of Senator Kyle questioning why the Federal Government should be paying the bills of such public servants. Leave it to the (liberal) state of New York (that we can't hope to win in 2012) to pay for the bills. It's a state issue! It's a local issue! Don't bother us with this! We've gotta catch a plane to get home before Christmas!

Give me a damned break!

I was in day two of a brand new job I had when the planes hit the World Trade Center, the Pentagon, and the cornfield in Pennsylvania. I remember very poignantly the outpouring of support that came from all corners of the United States. Cleaning up Ground Zero was a much bigger job than the city of New York could be asked to tackle. I know groups of firefighters who left their homes in New England and drove to New York asking what they could do to help. I know there had to be firefighters who came from all of these great 50 states, and I am sure as I write this that there must be public servants from around America whose health has suffered because of the contaminants they inhaled following this attack.

So Senator Kyl, are you really simply a dunderhead or are you one of the most tight-fisted Scrooges ever to serve in the Senate? Here's your rope Senator! Make sure it's secured good and tight, just like you.

Civil Rights Integration Wasn't So Bad

Gov. Haley Barbour, of that bastion of liberalism known as Mississippi, wanted to be the next President of the United States. Problem is, there's a black man in the White House, so if you want to appear to be mainstream, you have to try to look, well, mainstream. So Gov. Barbour was clearly trying to position himself in the center, at least on the race issue, in hopes that he might appear to be a palatable alternative in the general election.

A few months ago, I remember hearing Gov. Barbour talking about how the desegregation of Mississippi wasn't all that painful, as he, himself, had been part of a desegregated high school. Well, turns out Gov. Barbour misspoke on that point, as the high school he attended was not desegregated until years after he graduated. Maybe it just felt like it was desegregated.

Now, this is the gist of the report I heard on MSNBC earlier, as Gov. Barbour attempts to rewrite history by saying that his recollection of the desegregation of the south wasn't all that bad.

Wasn't all that bad? Maybe for a good ol' boy from

46

Mississippi, the civil rights era might not have been all that bad. I'm sure Martin Luther King would disagree Gov. Barbour!

So Haley, here's your rope. You won't have to tighten it much, since you've got so much flab under that dunderhead of yours!

Privatize Everything

I just had the most brilliant idea! I was thinking about the issue of what services government should provide, and I came up with this awesome inspiration! After giving this matter extensive thought, I think that we should privatize everything the government does today!

Think about it! Wouldn't it be just awesome if we could tell all the generals they are no longer in the employ of the United States Government, but they had been transferred to the employment of the arms industry? We would no longer need to argue over how much of the Federal budget should be devoted to nuclear weapons versus social services.

Social Security? Forget it! It's gone! Everyone should just fend for themselves, and that's a great idea because those financial wizards on Wall Street (you know, the ones who know *everything* there is to know about finances) will be in charge. Who needs financial regulators? We live in the great U.S. of A.! The purest free market economy in the world! Without laws to regulate what is appropriate for the captains of industry to do, why they should be able to make so much money, and as we all know, when we let the rich get richer, of course they will allow some of the profits trickle down to the rest of us. They're such a compassionate bunch, you know!

Health care? We'll let the insurance industry run that show. It's in their interest to have as many people covered as possible, isn't it? So of course they will be benevolent leaders and only charge us what is fair.

Let's see, who would agree with this idea? I have to guess that Sharon Angle would think this is an awesome idea. After all, with the military disbanded, all her supporters would be free to lock and load to pursue those "Second Amendment remedies" without fear of stepping on the military's toes.

All those right wing militia groups should be able to breathe a great big sigh of relief too. After all, aren't most of them training for the day that the vaunted United States military launches an attack against them? Without a military, they would become the bad boys!

The best part about this plan is that in less than a week, you will have the opportunity to implement it. On Tuesday, November 2, 2010, if you like this plan pull the lever and vote for any candidate with an R next to his or her name. They'll cut your taxes so low that they won't be able to pay for anything, except their salaries, of course.

Armageddon on Wall Street

Wall Street Turmoil Boosts Obama

John McCain had a pretty rough week. I'm sure that when he launched his falsely indignant attack against Barack Obama for the latter's speaking of pigs and lipstick, he must have felt good about the flow of the campaign to that point. But there were storm clouds brewing on the economic horizon, and this could not bode well for a candidate who, by his own admission, is not strong on the economy. Over the weekend, we were wondering who was going to buy Lehman Brothers, as the company looked for a buyer. By Monday, though, the picture looked much worse, as Lehman Brothers filed for Chapter 11 bankruptcy. We also learned that all was not well with Merrill Lynch, which was not a surprise to me.

What was a surprise to me, however, was the news that insurance giant AIG was failing, and an even greater surprise was that the federal government was loaning AIG $85 billion, so they could stay afloat.

Given John McCain's propensity to try to distance

51

himself from Bush Administration snafus, this would have seemed to be the time to stick with his maverick image. Instead, what did McCain do? He threw out a long record of anti-regulation by proposing a new bureaucrat to regulate banks that provide mortgages. That flip flop got the attention of pundits who jumped all over it.

Apparently not satisfied with how his proposal was playing out, McCain decided it was time to play economic tough guy, by declaring that if he were President, he would fire the head of the Securities Exchange Commission, who, McCain alleged, serves at the "pleasure of the President." I can only imagine that McCain thought he had a great sound clip there, at least until the media revealed that his information is incorrect. You see, the SEC is an independent body, and while it is true that the President nominates an individual to fill the post when it is vacant, the President does not have the authority to fire the person. Now, the average guy on the street may not know who fires the SEC Chairman, but John McCain is not an ordinary man on the street. He's a guy who is aspiring to be the leader of the free world, in the highest office in the land. I think it's reasonable to expect that such a man would know details like this.

So What Is McCain to Do?

So this puts McCain in a very difficult position. Either he knew his information was inaccurate and he lied to us because he wanted to make a good impression, or he is as out of touch on economic matters as Barack Obama and others have been saying all along. So now McCain's having a really hard time. Your post-convention bounce is history, and some polls are showing Obama has passed you. What's a desperate politician to do? Of course! Get together with Sarah Palin! It's worked before!

I can only imagine how McCain must have felt when Palin introduced him as her running mate, or how he must have felt when she slipped up and referred to a future "Palin and McCain Administration." John McCain has seen his star fall so quickly that he is rendering himself irrelevant as long as the economy is issue number one with the American public. With financial Armageddon rampaging on Wall Street, about the only way an issue could leap frog into the forefront would be a major international crisis or,

God forbid, another terror attack on American soil.

Barack Obama, meanwhile, has a golden opportunity to seal the deal on this election by presenting his plan for how the Obama Administration would handle this crisis. Such an exercise would not be purely academic, because the likelihood is that when he takes office in January (we hope) the economic problems that exist today will still be there for him to tackle.

A piece of that plan has already been unveiled, in terms of the tax plan Obama envisions (a tax cut for every taxpayer who makes $250,000 or less). Such a plan makes sense, if a tax cut proposal does make sense, because it gives the tax breaks to the vast majority of the American public, who can really stimulate the economy.

As this election heads into the homestretch, Obama has the opportunity to build a solid coalition that will propel him into history. He needs to take advantage of the opportunities that present themselves between now and November 4.

Is Sarah Palin Ready For Prime Time?

I wrote this story during President Obama's first presidential campaign, and at the time, Sarah Palin was the talk all across the country. People were just starting to ask questions about her viability as a candidate, though, setting aside questions about whether she was actually ready to serve in office, if elected vice president. Mid-way through President Obama's second term, people are still asking whether Palin is ready for prime time yet!

The major party candidates have chosen their running mates and we now have insights into priorities and thought processes of Senator Barack Obama and Senator John McCain.

Obama chose a six-term Senator, Joe Biden, who is respected on both sides of the aisle on matters pertaining to foreign policy. He's run for President twice, in this year's contest until Iowa and back in 1988. Even President Bush has called upon Biden for his insights on matters related to foreign policy. He is, in short, extremely qualified to step in as President and Commander-in-Chief, should the unthinkable happen to President Obama.

Now let's look at McCain. He's been labeled a war hero for having gotten himself shot down in Vietnam and subsequently imprisoned by the Viet Cong. So far as I can remember, no other President has been in a Vietnamese prison camp, which either means that all other Presidents elected since Vietnam have been unqualified, or we should not presume that McCain is qualified to be Commander-in-Chief simply because he has.

Obviously Sen. McCain feels he is sufficiently qualified to be Commander-in-Chief because he chose Gov. Sarah Palin to be his running mate. So what does Gov. Palin bring to the Republican ticket? It's obvious, isn't it?

It now appears that Sen. John McCain, a desert-dweller from Arizona, is well-positioned to win the state that is the epitome of the Great White North, Alaska.

I mean, that's got to be the strategy, right? It's the only plausible reason why McCain, a man, could choose a woman with so little experience like Gov. Palin, right? I mean, McCain's a bright enough guy, isn't he? He wouldn't have chosen someone like Sarah Palin to serve in the second highest office in the land simply to attempt to woo some of Hillary Clinton's 18 million votes to his side, right? No way. McCain's smarter than that. He couldn't be expecting all those liberal pro-choice women to set aside that issue to vote for him, just because his anti-choice running mate is a woman, right?

He couldn't be thinking that all those people who voted for Hillary in the primaries would suddenly decide to vote for him and his NRA card carrying running mate even though many of them are in favor of sensible gun control. He wouldn't be thinking that? He would never be **that** small-minded, right?

McCain couldn't be expecting all those environmentally concerned Democrats to suddenly throw caution to the wind and say, "Yeah, let's vote for McCain, who supports off-shore drilling, and his running mate who supports drilling in the Alaskan National Wildlife Refuge," just because she's a woman?

Here's the only problem. McCain is a Republican, and I've lived under the premise that if Republicans were smart they would be Democrats. Need proof? What did Papa Bush say about his son after he stole the 2000 election? Something to the effect of being proud of Boy

George because he proved it was possible for a C student to make something of himself! Something tells me that if, in fact, George W. Bush was a C student, his dad had to talk to the professors to pump up his score!

It makes you wonder what McCain thinks about the American people. Does he think that American women are so shallow that they would choose to vote for McCain and Palin simply because of her gender? Common sense would dictate this was not the case, because the majority of American voters are women, so if all women marched in lockstep behind their gender's icons, some of them would have been elected President by now.

Hit OPEC Where It Counts

I'm going to address this article to Sen. Obama, mostly since we know the John "Shoot From The Hip" McCain doesn't have a diplomatic bone in his body, and because it is my expectation Obama will next be known as President Obama.

Mr. President, you've just taken office. Gasoline prices, even in the dead of winter, are sitting around $4 a gallon, and many of the people who voted for you in November are hurting. Tackling the cost of gasoline is one of your highest priorities, so what are you going to do?

If you don't mind some advice, here's what I would do. I would immediately convene a summit somewhere in the middle east and tell the OPEC nations that gas prices at $4.00 a gallon is tantamount to declaring war not only on the United States, but on the rest of the civilized world.

My first thought, when I conceptualized this article, was that we should tell OPEC that until crude oil prices drop to, say, $40 per barrel, we'll cut off all foreign aid to all OPEC nations. But then I did a little Google search and found an article that talked about that very idea. The problem is that most of the oil rich nations do not receive any foreign aid from the United States, so that's not much of a bargaining chip to throw on the table.

But then I found an interesting quotation from former Representative Lee Hamilton, in an article in the CBS News archives titled "Public Enemy #1: OPEC." (http://www.cbsnews.com/stories/2000/06/23/politics/main 209161.shtml)

"We can't approach the middle east simply as an oil problem and try to threaten all of these countries that are friends and allies of ours, whose support we need in order to keep Saddam Hussein in the box, in order for the peace process to go forward," former Rep. Hamilton was quoted as saying.

That quote was made back in 2000, before Osama bin Laden attacked the U.S., before the U.S. attacked the Taliban, and before Boy George Bush lied us into a war against Saddam Hussein. In fact, correct me if I'm wrong, but didn't the U.S. depose Hussein? Didn't we do it without help from these OPEC nations? And didn't the Iraqi "government" already execute him? Yeah, I thought so.

So while the august Representative Hamilton's

quote may have made sense in 2000, does it still make sense? What have the OPEC nations, particularly those in the Middle East, done for us lately? How valuable are they as allies if they were not even willing to join us in the ill-fated war against Iraq?

In short, it seems to me that there must be something that we have that the OPEC nations want, whether it be military aid or some other incentive that we can say to them, "You're not going to soak us for $140 a barrel for oil and expect us to keep our end of the pipeline flowing."

I don't expect OPEC to roll over and play dead just because President Obama threatens to cut them off. I fully expect they will continue to manipulate the supply of oil as long as they can in order to keep gas and crude oil prices as high as possible for as long as possible. If that is the case, my suggestion to you, Mr. President, would be to take every last dollar that you can squeeze out of those countries and send it right back to the American people, so we can afford to drive to work.

How Does the USA Presidential Election System Work?

The reality is that we do not have a Presidential election. We have 50 individual elections, one for each of the states. And when you go to the polls and vote for the candidate of your choice, you are not actually voting for that candidate but for an elector whose job it is is to decide who should be the President of the United States. The electors collectively are known as the Electoral College. This, in my opinion, should be eliminated. It was conceptualized by the founding fathers, under the premise that the American people in 18th century USA were not sufficiently educated to handle the responsibility of choosing the President of the United States directly.

If, in fact, it is true that some 238 years after the signing of the Declaration of Independence we are still sufficiently illiterate and uneducated that we can't choose our leader ourselves, then there is a problem with the American educational system that is far greater than ever imagined.

This scenario can result in a situation where a

candidate can have more votes from common, every day Americans and still lose the election. Witness Al Gore, for instance. If the Electoral College had been abolished, Al Gore would have been President, not Boy George, and several thousand of our soldiers would not be dead today.

I'm getting off topic a tad bit. The bottom line is that whichever candidate can get 270 electoral votes on election night in November will be the President of the United States, and it matters little whether that person has the support of the majority of Americans.

The Debate That Almost Wasn't

Both Candidates Exceed Expectations

OK, I've got to admit that I was really looking forward to the first of three Presidential debates because I was so looking forward to watching John McCain crash and burn in a most inspirational way. I mean, with the erratic way McCain had been behaving the past couple of weeks leading up to the debate, such a scenario was plausible. Unfortunately, I didn't get what I was seeking. And so McCain, whose campaign was teetering on the very edge of a deep, dark abyss, has managed to find stable ground, for now.

That's not to say, John, that I think you have successfully righted the ship. Not by a long shot, because I also believe that Barack Obama performed better than I had expected. So I don't see you gaining in the polls, based solely on your performance.

Both candidates had their high points and low points. I'll start with Barack Obama, but don't worry

The World According to Crash Politics, Money & Stuff!

John...I've got plenty for you!

Barack, my friend, I've got to remind you that John McCain is the enemy here, and his Republican handlers will use your words against you eight days a week! So next time, please, please, please, please, PLEASE do not talk about how "right" McCain is about anything, even if you follow up such comments with contrasting information that was your main message any way! I mean, you may have scored a few points for diplomacy, but I can just imagine Karl Rove and his henchmen giggling with glee as the video editor was cutting and splicing your words to put into their advertisement that was released immediately after the debate. We don't need to give them anything they can shoot in your direction.

On the other hand, Obama did send a message to voters who previously considered him to be too soft on international affairs. He correctly reminded Americans that it was Osama Bin Laden who ordered the attacks in New York and Washington, D.C., and made it very clear that he would go to any length (including crossing the border between Afghanistan and Pakistan to capture and "kill" Bin Laden, if the Pakistani government was unwilling or unable to do so.) I was particularly moved by his use of the word kill, because if Obama were truly too soft, he would simply say capture, leaving the door open that Bin Laden could live.

Obama also came off as much more diplomatic than McCain. While Obama discussed the need for top-level diplomacy between the United States and rogue regimes such as Iran, North Korea and Venezuela he reminded everyone that McCain was seen singing "Bomb Iran." Yes, John, we saw you smirk after that gaffe, but we also noticed that you did not respond to that barb.

Now let's talk about McCain. I can't be the only one who noticed that McCain could not bring himself to even glance at Obama during this debate, even as the two men shook hands before and after the debate. It made McCain look inflexible, rigid, and not just a bit childish, as it reminded me of my two oldest children who fight like cats and dogs.

There was inconsistency in McCain's message too. On one hand, he tried to paint the picture of Obama having the most liberal voting record in the Senate (a charge they also leveled against John Kerry four years ago) but later trying to compare Barack Obama to George Bush! McCain said Obama's inflexibility to believe that the surge in Iraq was working reminds him of Bush. Obama, wisely, countered with the fact that McCain has supported the President with 90 percent of his votes over the past eight years.

There was a bit of role reversal going on, too. Going into the debate, pundits cautioned that Obama should not be too professorial, talking down to McCain. However, McCain tried time and time again to suggest that Obama doesn't understand various nuances of foreign policy, and the more often he tried that tactic, it seemed that he was the one who was preaching. Obama, meanwhile, seemed to be in command of his information, which made me feel comfortable that Obama would not be a foreign policy liability, like George W. Bush.

All-in-all, I think both candidates came away from the debate with enough to feel good about, but each wishing they could have hit the proverbial home run on multiple occasions. In the end, I believe Obama scored a victory because his standing in the polls has not suffered in the aftermath of this debate. As I write this, CNN's poll of polls has Obama leading 48 to 43 with 9 percent undecided. CBS/New York Times has Obama leading 47 to 42 with 11 percent undecided. Even the rabidly conservative Fox News poll has Obama leading 45 to 39 with 16 percent undecided. Lastly, CNN reports the latest Marist College poll has Obama with 49, McCain with 44 and 7 percent undecided.

There's another good reason why I feel optimistic about Obama's chances on November 4, and that is because Sarah Palin gets to go up against Joe Biden on Thursday. I can hardly wait!

Refusing Federal Aid the Peak of Irresponsibility

Imagine this scenario. There are 50 states in our great nation. The governors of Texas, Mississippi, Louisiana, Alaska, South Carolina and Idaho are all concerned about whether they should accept economic stimulus money from the Obama Administration. Coincidentally, Obama is a Democrat, the only members of the House who voted in favor of this legislation are Democrats, and only three Republican Senators voted in favor of the bill. Now factor in the detail that all of the aforementioned governors are Republican.

Keeping all these details in mind, do you buy the fact that these Republican governors are not putting their own ideologies over the needs of the constituents they serve?

It must be stressed that as of this moment, none of the governors have actually rejected the funds, but all six are said to be considering it, for a variety of reasons. In political parlance, this is called a trial balloon. Politicians float a trial balloon to see what the public response is, and then make a decision.

I am quite sure that there are many people in the states of Texas, Mississippi, Louisiana, Alaska, South Carolina and Idaho who cheered when Congress passed this important legislation, because one thing has become abundantly clear that people in every state of our country are suffering because of the poor economy former President Bush turned over to President Obama.

Imagine being someone who lives in one of those six states who is about to lose their home because they are unemployed, and their governor decides he doesn't want to accept these funds. You might be upset, if you were such a person.

I believe these governors need to hear from their citizens. In order to help facilitate that process, I have gone to all six of the states' websites and found contact information for each governor's office. If you do decide to write to your governor, I would be most pleased if you could send a copy of it to me at authorjimhenry@gmail.com?

It should be noted that as I continue to research this issue, I have found that the governor of Idaho has actually issued an executive order on the process that his state agencies must do in order to request funds from this bill.

Here's An Interesting Angle

I'm still reveling in the afterglow of the Obama inauguration, so I hope you'll excuse me if I'm not thinking too much about the 2012 Presidential Election. Add to that the fact that I already know who I will be supporting in four years, I did not immediately recognize that each of these Governors are being touted in GOP circles as potential Presidential candidates. That, in and of itself, may not seem like a smoking gun, but here's something else I've learned.

It seems that Rep. James Clyburn (D-SC), anticipating that his Governor would refuse to accept bailout funds, included in the stimulus legislation a provision that would allow state legislatures to override any decision made by a governor not to accept bailout funds. So now Sanford & Company can all grand stand against this law, based on fiscal irresponsibility (solidifying themselves as conservatives, which will certain endear them to the Republican base), and at the same time know that the state Legislatures will rise to the occasion and accept the funds, even if they may be holding their noses as they vote. Talk about having your cake and eating it too!

Of course, if it does come to pass that all six of these governors refuse to accept the funds, and then any one of them (or all of them) do wind up running for President in 4 years, they will have to explain to the voters of not just their state but all 50 states why they put their own political ideologies and Presidential ambitions ahead of the working men and women who would benefit most from this legislation.

Hillary, You're Not TR!

Do the Right Thing Hillary

In 1912, former President Theodore Roosevelt ran for the presidency against William Howard Taft and Woodrow Wilson. Throughout his political life, including two terms as President (one elected and one filling out almost all of William McKinley's second term) Roosevelt had been a Republican. After hand-picking Taft as his successor, Taft had proven to be an abysmal failure, by Roosevelt's estimation, which prompted him to come out of retirement and try to unseat him. Now, Roosevelt was no fool. He knew how the game was played, and he knew that if he failed to secure the Republican nomination, he would stand no chance to regain the White House. In those days, the idea of having a Direct Primary, as many states do today, was a very new concept. In many states, delegates to the party's convention were chosen by political bosses, and most of those bosses lined up behind Taft. As a result, when Republicans met in convention in the summer of 1912, Taft

74

had a steamroller ready to pummel Roosevelt, who had won the majority of delegates available in Direct Primaries, but had lost in the other states.

Roosevelt could have chosen to go away quietly, but he chose instead to press onward. Whether it was vindictiveness or vanity, I'll never know, but Roosevelt and his supporters bolted from the convention and convened elsewhere. The decision was made to form a new political party, known officially as the National Progressive Party. It came to be known as the Bull Moose Party after a reporter asked Roosevelt how he was feeling, and his response was "Bully as a Bull Moose."

By the fall of 1912, Roosevelt and Taft combined for more electoral votes and more popular votes than Wilson did, but neither could hope to win enough votes to overtake Wilson as long as the other was still in the race. Taft won the nomination under the rules that existed in that day and age, and as the incumbent, he had every right to remain in the race. If Roosevelt had merely stepped aside in 1912, Taft would have won that election, and Roosevelt would have been the odds on favorite to win the nomination and the election in 1916.

Instead, Roosevelt pressed onward, and he sunk Taft's reelection bid, putting himself at odds with the Republican base. Essentially, he torpedoed his own career and Taft's at the same time.

Now we're about a century in the future and we have a similar problem brewing. Barack Obama just made history tonight by securing enough delegates to win the Democratic nomination for President. You can say he did it by winning in states that Democrats have little or no chance of winning in November, while Hillary won the states Democrats have to win in order to have a fighting chance. But the fact remains, Senator Clinton, you lost. End of story. Now the question is, will you step aside gracefully and concede that under the rules that exist today, Barack Obama won the nomination?

She certainly didn't sound like that when she gave her speech tonight. Instead, she sounds like a candidate who really believes that she can win it all in November. If she lets her ego get in the way of good old fashioned common sense, she'll stick around as a thorn in Barack Obama's side until the convention, and when she's faced with the reality that Obama has the nomination in his pocket, she's going to have a decision to make.

Will she make the decision Roosevelt made and torpedo Obama's chances of winning the White House? If she does, she certainly will be torpedoing her own chances of winning the nomination in 4 or 8 years.

Do the right thing Hillary. Tell your supporters that we as Democrats ought to get along at least as well as we would with your average Republican. Get behind Barack Obama because it's the right thing to do for the country. If you do, almost certainly you will be rewarded with this prize you covet so sincerely. If you do not, America will suffer and your career will be over.

We Need FDR's Style of Getting Things Done

How Did FDR Do It?

I am a student of history, and studied 20th Century American History as part of my master's degree studies. One of the most fascinating and perhaps controversial figures of the century had to be President Franklin Delano Roosevelt.

Roosevelt was a Democrat, and a cousin of the Republican President Theodore Roosevelt. FDR, however, was truly not ideologically driven. He didn't aspire to advance a particular agenda when he took office in 1933. Instead, he sought to get America going again, after suffering through four years of the Great Depression.

I've been thinking a lot about what I learned about FDR lately, because of the media's propensity to sensationalize our current economic plight by comparing what we are experiencing today to the Great Depression.

One of the stories I read in a biography of Roosevelt was his rather unique way of bringing together ideologically opposed people from Congress and literally force them to compromise and give him a bill he could sign.

Here's how he did it. Roosevelt would identify the key players in a piece of legislation, and he would summon them to the White House. Once they arrived, he would take them into a room, and tell them that he would not allow them to leave the room until they had compromised and given him a program that he could sign into law. Then he would leave the room, shut the door, and lock it from the outside. He would literally hold these people hostage in this room, but the results were amazing. Given such a set of circumstances, you would be amazed how quickly these ideologues would set their philosophical differences aside and come up with a bill to present to Congress.

Sometimes, when I think about the fundamental differences of opinion on what will stimulate economic growth that exist today, I wish President Obama would invite Republican House Minority Leader John Boehner, Senate Minority Leader Mitch McConnell, Speaker of the House Nancy Pelosi and Senate President Harry Reid to the White House, ostensibly to have tea and discuss how we can bring these two hostile forces together for the good of the country. And once they're all there ready to chat, to have President Obama stand up and say:

"Madam Speaker, gentlemen, I have a busy agenda ahead of me today, so I apologize I must excuse myself. The last item I have on my daily schedule is to review your compromise legislation on the economic stimulus package. See you tonight!" Then, of course, he would need to lock the door from the outside.

Can you imagine Nancy Pelosi? I can just picture her hammering on the door, screaming to be let out, while

White House staffers snigger in the hallway outside, standing alongside the Secret Service agents who were assigned to make sure no one let them out without Obama's permission.

Do you think we would end up with a stimulus package in a day? I bet so. Do you think it would be loaded with pork, especially if they knew the more creative they became in defining what would actually stimulate the economy, the longer they would have to stay in that locked room?

I can just imagine Boehner screaming that he needed to get out to go to the bathroom, while White House staffers out in the hallway suggest that he work a little faster, or perhaps try crossing his legs.

Do you think we could get these ideologues to set aside their petty differences for the good of the country if dinner came and went without food being delivered under the doorway?

I can just imagine Harry Reid making an impassioned plea for mercy, saying that his blood sugar was dropping so low that he was unable to think straight. I can just imagine White House Chief of Staff Rahm Emanuel speaking through the still-locked door, asking about their level of progress on the Legislation (while chowing down on dinner out in the hallway.)

Do you think we could get these nitwits to agree on the level of the tax cut, who would get it, and whether they would apply the cut to 2008 income, so the average taxpayers would benefit more quickly in the form of a larger than expected income tax return?

I can just imagine McConnell grumbling something about "high crimes and misdemeanors" and "initiating impeachment proceedings" as they hand the grinning President Obama the completed legislation when he returns 12 hours after he first left them.

It kind of makes me wonder if they can lock the doors to the Senate and House Chambers from the outside..........

Bush's Bailout Legislation

You Won't Believe Your Eyes

Those of us who are interested in the machinations of the Universe inside the beltway have heard lawmakers level charges about not having the time to read all the details in the monstrous pieces of legislation that goes before Congress. This will not be a problem with the recently filed legislation that is designed to bail out the nation's banking industry from the mistakes they made that has our economy on the brink of collapse.

That was my chief concern when I heard that the Bush Administration was throwing together legislation to address the banking crisis. I couldn't imagine how they could address all the issues that led to the collapse of Lehman Brothers, AIG, Bear Stearns and Merrill Lynch. Now I can see how they did it.

They didn't.

You do not have to have a law degree from an

accredited university to read the legislation the Bush Administration sent to Congress and understand what is going on. Just as the Bush Administration seized the opportunity to solidify its power after 9/11, the thief-in-chief is trying to use this latest debacle, which really is an indictment of the Republican economic philosophy, and come out of this with even greater power. Essentially, the administration is seeking $700,000,000,000 that we the people will pay for long after he has left office, with no strings attached.

Don't believe it? I've got the text of the bill that was sent to Congress, along with messages that essentially say, "You better hurry up and pass this because if you don't, we're going to blame you when the s%^t hits the fan."

Draft Bailout Plan

LEGISLATIVE PROPOSAL FOR TREASURY AUTHORITY TO PURCHASE MORTGAGE-RELATED ASSETS

Section 1. Short Title.

This Act may be cited as _____.

Sec. 2. Purchases of Mortgage-Related Assets.

(a) Authority to Purchase.--The Secretary is authorized to purchase, and to make and fund commitments to purchase, on such terms and conditions as determined by the Secretary, mortgage-related assets from any financial institution having its headquarters in the United States.

(b) Necessary Actions.--The Secretary is authorized to take such actions as the Secretary deems necessary to carry out the authorities in this Act, including, without limitation:

(1) appointing such employees as may be required to carry out the authorities in this Act and defining their duties;

(2) entering into contracts, including contracts for services authorized by section 3109 of title 5, United States Code, without regard to any other provision of law regarding public contracts;

(3) designating financial institutions as financial agents of the Government, and they shall perform all such reasonable duties related to this Act as financial agents of

the Government as may be required of them;

(4) establishing vehicles that are authorized, subject to supervision by the Secretary, to purchase mortgage-related assets and issue obligations; and

(5) issuing such regulations and other guidance as may be necessary or appropriate to define terms or carry out the authorities of this Act.

Sec. 3. Considerations.

In exercising the authorities granted in this Act, the Secretary shall take into consideration means for--

(1) providing stability or preventing disruption to the financial markets or banking system; and

(2) protecting the taxpayer.

Sec. 4. Reports to Congress.

Within three months of the first exercise of the authority granted in section 2(a), and semiannually thereafter, the Secretary shall report to the Committees on the Budget, Financial Services, and Ways and Means of the House of Representatives and the Committees on the Budget, Finance, and Banking, Housing, and Urban Affairs of the Senate with respect to the authorities exercised under this Act and the considerations required by section 3.

Sec. 5. Rights; Management; Sale of Mortgage-Related Assets.

(a) Exercise of Rights.--The Secretary may, at any time, exercise any rights received in connection with mortgage-related assets purchased under this Act.

(b) Management of Mortgage-Related Assets.--The Secretary shall have authority to manage mortgage-related assets purchased under this Act, including revenues and portfolio risks therefrom.

(c) Sale of Mortgage-Related Assets.--The Secretary may, at any time, upon terms and conditions and at prices determined by the Secretary, sell, or enter into securities loans, repurchase transactions or other financial transactions in regard to, any mortgage-related asset purchased under this Act.

(d) Application of Sunset to Mortgage-Related Assets.--The authority of the Secretary to hold any mortgage-related asset purchased under this Act before the termination date in section 9, or to purchase or fund the purchase of a mortgage-related asset under a commitment entered into before the termination date in section 9, is not subject to the provisions of section 9.

87

Sec. 6. Maximum Amount of Authorized Purchases.

The Secretary's authority to purchase mortgage-related assets under this Act shall be limited to $700,000,000,000 outstanding at any one time

Sec. 7. Funding.

For the purpose of the authorities granted in this Act, and for the costs of administering those authorities, the Secretary may use the proceeds of the sale of any securities issued under chapter 31 of title 31, United States Code, and the purposes for which securities may be issued under chapter 31 of title 31, United States Code, are extended to include actions authorized by this Act, including the payment of administrative expenses. Any funds expended for actions authorized by this Act, including the payment of administrative expenses, shall be deemed appropriated at the time of such expenditure.

Sec. 8. Review.

Decisions by the Secretary pursuant to the authority of this Act are non-reviewable and committed to agency discretion, and may not be reviewed by any court of law or any administrative agency.

Sec. 9. Termination of Authority.

The authorities under this Act, with the exception of authorities granted in sections 2(b)(5), 5 and 7, shall terminate two years from the date of enactment of this Act.

Sec. 10. Increase in Statutory Limit on the Public Debt.

Subsection (b) of section 3101 of title 31, United States Code, is amended by striking out the dollar limitation contained in such subsection and inserting in lieu thereof $11,315,000,000,000.

Sec. 11. Credit Reform.

The costs of purchases of mortgage-related assets made under section 2(a) of this Act shall be determined as provided under the Federal Credit Reform Act of 1990, as applicable.

Sec. 12. Definitions.

For purposes of this section, the following definitions shall apply:

(1) Mortgage-Related Assets.--The term "mortgage-related assets" means residential or commercial mortgages and any securities, obligations, or other instruments that are based on or related to such mortgages, that in each case was originated or issued on or before September 17, 2008.

(2) Secretary.--The term "Secretary" means the Secretary of the Treasury.

(3) United States.--The term "United States" means the States, territories, and possessions of the United States and the District of Columbia.

What Does This Mean?

When I pasted the text of this law into my word processor, it revealed that the word count of this $700 billion legislation is 870 words. I wrote longer term papers as an undergraduate student in college! Do you know what that means? If we attached a dollar amount to every word in this document, the value of each word would be $804,597,701 and some loose change. That makes the bailout of AIG look fiscally conservative! I can't be the only one who is thinking that Boy George and his Merry Band of Neocons have been abducted by aliens and replaced with aliens whose goal is to run the United States of America into the ground!

So let's take a look at the details of this legislation that is so important that Bush Administration officials urged

Congress to pass without amendment. The first provision that really jumps out at me reads:

"(3) designating financial institutions as financial agents of the Government, and they shall perform all such reasonable duties related to this Act as financial agents of the Government as may be required of them;"

So what does this mean? It means that the Bush Administration is asking Congress to allow them to hire (and presumably pay) financial agents from many of the same companies the legislation is designed to bail out to make decisions about how this money should be spent.

YOU HAVE GOT TO BE KIDDING ME!

These yahoos in Washington, D.C. must really believe Americans are stupid, or just too lazy to find out the truth before the law is passed. I mean, it was a tremendous miscarriage of justice when Bush and Cheney brought their oil baron tycoons into the White House to set energy policy for their administration (which resulted in skyrocketing fuel costs, mind you.)

Let's see other ways they plan to put the screws to the American public, shall we? Here's another nifty little picture:

91

Sec. 6. Maximum Amount of Authorized Purchases.

"The Secretary's authority to purchase mortgage-related assets under this Act shall be limited to $700,000,000,000 *outstanding at any one time."*

What this means, friends, is that the $700 billion price tag is not really the price tag. It means that if the government buys the defaulted mortgage from a bank, letting said bank off the hook, but then turns around and sells that property, the proceeds of that sale can be put back into the coffers for the Treasury Department to play with again. Depending upon how many properties Uncle Sam unloads, they could create essentially a revolving fund that only the Treasury Secretary can access. Here's another wonderful provision in this law that should send shock waves through anyone who loves liberty:

"Sec. 8. Review.

Decisions by the Secretary pursuant to the authority of this Act are non-reviewable and committed to agency discretion, and may not be reviewed by any court of law or any administrative agency."

This section essentially names Treasury Secretary Henry Paulson the Dictator of these funds, because there is no means of recourse to challenge any decision he makes. To say that the administration is essentially saying, "Trust me," is ludicrous.

What's The Bottom Line?

The bottom line here, my friends, is that there is a financial crisis here, but the legislation the administration has advanced does absolutely nothing to benefit the consumers and homeowners who are suffering. This bill is all about lining the pockets of the entrenched powers, giving absolute authority to the Treasury Secretary who no one aside from the U.S. Senate had the opportunity to vote for, and doing so in the backdrop of a presidential election.

The Republican Party has been in control of the White House for the past eight years. They controlled Congress for most of that time. John McCain was a champion of deregulation, at least until last week when it became apparent to everyone that deregulation in the banking industry is what led to this collapse. And now the Republican Administration wants to have you and I pay for the sins of the Wall Street bankers, while not offering one iota of help to the families that are suffering.

If it's Broke, FIX IT!

During the 2008 Election Cycle, someone at hubpages.com posed the following question, inviting hubbers to provide answers to the question. My response follows.

What will it take for Americans to truly fix their government, and how bad will it have to get to motivate them?

Leave it to Neocons to Sidestep The Issue

As I write this article, there has been one other response to this question. Typically, it's written by an ultra-conservative who can't resist the temptation to label anyone to his left as a communist. That's about as ridiculous as someone on the left suggesting that anyone to their right is a fascist. The reality is that Communism and Fascism are extremes, and liberals, progressives and conservatives fall somewhere in the middle.

One of the ways people on both sides of the political debate win elections is by painting their opponents as extremists. So when this guy refers to Barack Obama as a Communist, that's what he's trying to do. Similarly, if I called George Bush an ultraconservative neo-nazi fascist pig, and anyone whom he supports must therefore be a fascist as well, I would be guilty of the same "crime."

The basic question, though, speaks to a reality that at least in the writer's opinion, there is a problem, it's a big one, and it's got to be addressed. While I don't have a functioning crystal ball, I have a suspicion that once the Democrats can finally decide who their nominee will be, the country will begin to rally around that candidate. Why? Take a look at the issues.

The War In Iraq - This is a Republican nightmare. I'll give George Bush credit for trying to make the best out of a horrendous situation. First we were told that we were there looking for WMDs. Five years later, none have been found. Then we were told we were fighting the terrorists over there so we wouldn't have to fight them here. Problem is, they weren't there when we got there, so in that regard, things got worse by allowing them in, Then we were told that gas prices and oil prices in general would skyrocket if we didn't get matters under control. Well, gas prices

95

continue to skyrocket even with us there. Now they're telling us that things will get worse if we leave. Worse for who? We got rid of Saddam Hussein, now let's get out of there so we can stop being targets for the warring factions to shoot at.

It's The Economy Stupid - Let's face it, George Bush was never much of an economic success. He certainly didn't preside over the kind of growth that either Clinton or Reagan did. So he was already on shaky ground economically when the bubble burst in the housing market. You think people get antsy when they're afraid they'll lose their jobs? That's nothing compared with the fear people feel when they are afraid of losing their homes. Boy George tried to convince us that if Congress voted for tax cuts the economy would just take off. Now he's convinced that if you give 1,200 to a family with a couple of kids they're going to do their patriotic duty and go out and spend it all.

Instead, the majority of Americans are saying they plan to take those economic stimulus checks and pay off old bills. That's not going to stimulate the economy.

Plus, we've got John McCain admitting that he's not as well-informed on economic matters as he should be.

Thanks for being honest John, I'll give you that. The problem is that comments like that don't exactly inspire a lot of people who are hurting economically to vote for the likes of you.

Global Warming - There's probably still a good 30 percent of Americans who believe that Global Warming is a bunch of hocus pocus (the same 30 percent who think George Bush is doing a good job). The rest of us know there's something wrong.

Gas/Oil Prices - I touched on this earlier, but the problem with oil prices is so huge that it really needs its own headline here. High fuel costs are affecting so many areas of the economy. People who would normally take their kids to Disney World may have to think twice because the airlines aren't as affordable as they used to be, and the idea of driving with the rug rats when gas prices are floating around $3.50 a gallon on average is not terribly appealing.

Heating your home is a huge issue these days. Last month, near the end of the heating season, it cost my family more money to fill our oil tank than our rent. I predicted to my wife that it's only going to get worse, particularly if the

Republicans keep control of the White House. Did you ever think that a Texan would lift a finger to keep prices under control? Not with all those corporate big wigs funding his campaigns. Guess who they're supporting now?

Here's My Prediction - Sometime after the 10th of June, Democrats are going to settle on Barack Obama as the nominee, and Hillary Clinton will become his running mate. The economy will continue to head south, gas prices will continue to head north, and another 500-1000 of our brave soldiers will die by election day. With the exception of Barack leading our ticket with Hillary as Veep, I don't want the other scenarios to unfold. I just don't see Boy George and company actually doing anything to head them off at the pass.

Still, since there are still so many Republicans who would hold their nose and vote for any Republican before they would ever consider voting for a Democrat, the election will be close. Florida will be a Republican state, but Ohio will go to the Democrats, and Barack Obama will be elected President.

From the Ashes Comes the USS New York

In 1898, looking for a headline that could sell some

newspapers, William Randolph Hearst, owner of the *New York Sun,* told a journalist in Cuba to remain there, adding, "You furnish the pictures, I'll furnish the war."

This came in response to the sinking of the U.S.S. Maine. The subsequent outrage among the American public caused the now famous "Remember the Maine" rallying cry to be coined.

More than a century has passed since that phrase became popular, but I am reminded of the expression when I view pictures of the new battleship, the U.S.S. New York, whose motto is "Never Forget."

What makes this motto significant is how this ship came to be in existence. September 11, 2001 is undoubtedly one of the darkest days in American history. Muslim extremists hijacked several airplanes, two of which slammed into the twin towers of the World Trade Center. Subsequent to those impacts, of course we all know that the towers collapsed, killing thousands of Americans, many of whom were firefighters trying to clear the buildings.

In the years to come, work was performed to clean up the site, which had come to be known as "Ground Zero." But what became of the steel that had once gave form to the towers?

We can account for at least 24 tons of it when we look at the U.S.S. New York. Yes, it's true. In a classic thumbing of our collective nose at the likes of Osama bin Laden, we have built a battleship from the steel of the World Trade Center. What is particularly poignant is the purpose that this battleship exists to serve.

The U.S.S. New York will carry 360 sailors and 700 United States Marines, who will be prepared to go ashore using amphibious vehicles, designed to carry out anti-terrorist missions.

The chances of my dream coming true are remote at best, but I would love nothing more than to have crew from this glorious ship be responsible for capturing Osama bin Laden, and have him brought to U.S. soil on board the ship made of steel from the buildings he destroyed, along with thousands of innocent Americans.

With any luck, just as Americans still "Remember the Maine" more than 100 years after it was attacked, Americans in 2109 will Never Forget this beautiful ship, and the men and women who died so it could be created.

Evacuation Day - St. Patrick's Day Connection

In March of 1776, the British fleet departed Boston to go attack other areas, trying to keep those pesky colonists under control. Since this event happened in Boston Harbor, Bostonians claimed this as a holiday. The holiday is celebrated each year on March 17. That date should ring a bell with most folks, as the feast day of St. Patrick, the patron saint of Ireland. Boston has had a long standing association with Irish Catholics, and will continue to have that connection for the foreseeable future.

I used to work in municipal government for several communities in Western and Central Massachusetts. As municipal employees, state law guaranteed us the right to have 11 paid holidays a year, unless you happened to live in Suffolk County, where you were guaranteed 13 paid holidays. The same held true for all state employees, regardless of where they lived.

Evacuation Day was one of the two other holidays Boston area people got off with pay. The other extra one is Bunker Hill Day. A case could be made that Bunker Hill

Day would have more significance both to the city of Boston and to the United States in general, as Bunker Hill is associated with one of the more famous battles of the American Revolution. Ironically, even the Battle of Bunker Hill is somewhat of a misnomer, because historians will tell you that the Battle of Bunker Hill was actually fought on nearby Breed's Hill, but I guess folks decided Bunker Hill sounded better than Breed's Hill. But I digress.

As a municipal administrator, I used to argue that since all men (and women) are created equal, if municipal employees in Boston, Cambridge and Somerville got to celebrate Evacuation/St. Patrick's Day, all municipal employees should be treated equally.

The reason I ask the question about whether this is a real holiday is because of the event that inspired the holiday. The British and the Americans had been engaged in a stalemate for 11 months, with British ships sitting out in Boston Harbor. Only once Henry Knox arrived with upwards to 59 cannon (it's been said that cannon should not have an s even when pluralized), which were posted in position at Dorchester Heights was the stalemate broken.

A blog that commemorates this historic event,

located at http://boston1775.blogspot.com/2008/03/our.html quoted a British Officer who was reported to have said:

Our retreat was made this morning between the hours of two and eight. Our troops did not receive the smallest molestation, though the rebels were all night at work on the near hill, and we kept a constant fire upon them, from a battery of four twenty-four pounders. They did not return a single shot. It was lucky for the inhabitants now left in Boston they did not. For I am informed everything was prepared to set the town in a blaze had they fired one cannon.

Somehow I have a hard time buying that notion. Why, if the British were prepared to "set the town in a blaze" had they not done so during the previous 11 months during the stand-off? And why would they be retreating if they were in such a position? Further, why would the Americans not fire these cannon if they were under "a constant fire...from a battery of four twenty-four pounders," as the historic account contends?

Regardless of whose account you believe, the fact remains that the British did, in fact leave, and that there were no casualties reported on either side, so it begs the question, why is this holiday such a big deal?

I believe it is because of the connection with St. Patrick's Day. It would not be proper, in a nation that purports to value a separation of Church and State, to have an official holiday on a day in honor of a Saint. (You may argue that Christmas is such a holiday, but many others would argue that Christmas has become so commercialized that it is no longer a purely religious event). So in order to appease those who would object to such a holiday, they came up with the idea that it should be Evacuation Day, a great non-military victory, that apparently is only important enough that people in three eastern Massachusetts communities commemorate it.

I did some research to try to determine when this holiday became an official state holiday. Some report that Boston first celebrated Evacuation Day on March 17, 1901, some 125 years after the event. If it was such a momentous occasion, why would it take more than a century for the city to celebrate it?

I also found a copy of the Massachusetts General Law that pertains to Evacuation Day, the entire text of which follows:

Chapter 6: Section 12K. Evacuation Day

Section 12K. The governor shall annually issue a proclamation setting apart March seventeenth as Evacuation Day and recommending that it be observed by the people with appropriate exercises in the public schools and otherwise, as he may see fit, to the end that the first major military victory in the war for American independence, namely, the evacuation of Boston by the British, may be perpetuated.

I find it interesting that nowhere in that section does it refer to this being a holiday solely for Suffolk County, which begs the question of whether Gov. Deval Patrick could actually expand the scope of the observance to all 351 of the cities and towns in Massachusetts.

A little more research on this matter revealed that the influence of the holiday may be waning a bit, as the following excerpt from the Massachusetts General Laws would suggest:

SECTION 1. Notwithstanding section 12 and 13 of chapter 136 and chapter 71 of the General Laws and any other general or special law to the contrary, the school department of the city of Revere may, at the discretion of the school committee of the city, be open for business for all purposes including the instruction of students in classrooms on Thursday, March 17, 2005 and Friday, June 17, 2005.

SECTION 2. This act shall take effect upon its passage.

Approved March 15, 2005.

For the record, June 17 is the observance of the aforementioned Bunker Hill Day, so the lawmakers were not solely picking on Evacuation Day.

The fact that this holiday was not created for 125 years, and that it is now being watered down to allow local officials in Revere to decide whether their children should have to go to school or not would suggest to me that this holiday is really an event that is much more important to the Irish Americans than to the rest of the Commonwealth.

But fear not, ye Irish brethren. No one is planning to take away your God-given right to celebrate the departure of the British by drinking copious volumes of the poison of your choice in any Boston bar, pub, saloon or watering hole. Enjoy it! And have a drink for me, won't you?

A Soldier's Prayer

In Honor of Veterans' Day

If you know a veteran, say thank you for serving to preserve our freedoms! That is why I have published this hub! Thank you to all who have served!

Remember Our Troops

The World According to Crash Politics, Money & Stuff!

I just received a chain email asking to pass along pictures of our brave men and women in uniform, in honor of the supreme sacrifice many of them have made for us all. I didn't want to send this out by email to all my friends, because I suspect many do not read forwarded emails. However, the spirit of the request is noble, and so I have decided to publish these pictures on this hub, and at the bottom there is a prayer we can all say. Underneath the pictures, I've updated this page to include random thoughts the images inspire as I view them. If anyone has any thoughts of their own they would like to add, send them to authorjimhenry@gmail.com.

As I view this image, I wonder if this is a soldier returned from the war who is wondering through the field of his fallen comrades, or perhaps a man who has lost his brother, friend or sister?

The loss of American lives in the Iraq War is what makes my heart ache, particularly when I realize that the justification and benefits of this war are so small.

Can you imagine being these soldiers, seeing the coffins of their brothers and sisters in arms, wondering if they will be next to be draped in the flag?

Images like this are beautiful and present a sense of peacefulness. As I look at this picture, I feel a profound sense of hope that these brave people went to their graves proud of what they accomplished on behalf of us all.

As I view this procession, I can almost hear taps playing, taking this fallen hero to his final resting place. I may not know who you are, but I will never forget the sacrifice you have made for our country.

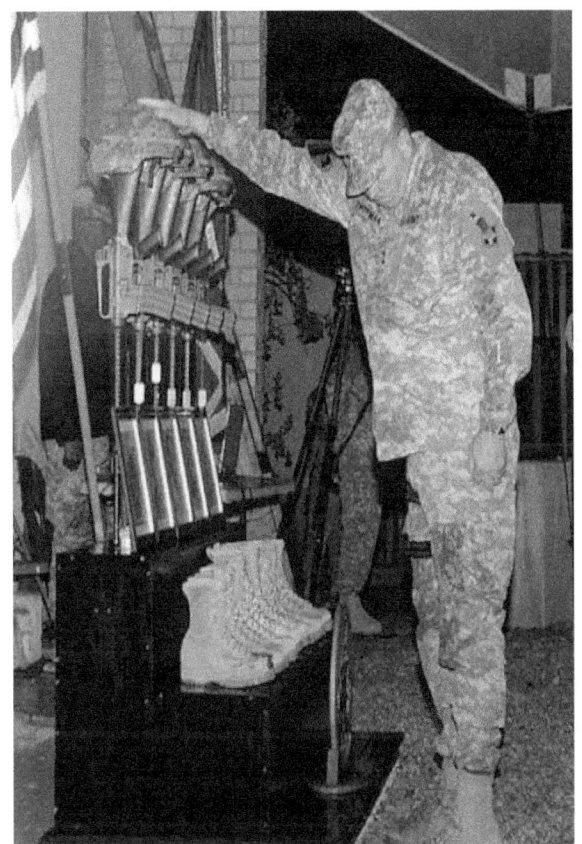

This must be a gut wrenching experience for the soldiers who are left behind. Still, the pain this man must be feeling is nothing compared with the weight of the sacrifice the soldiers who wore these boots and helmets gave for us all.

We'll never know who these men are thinking of while they stand in silence. It overwhelms me to think of how brave these fighting men and women are, going about the tasks others have decided for them, knowing that they could be next in line to go.

All I can think of, as I view the image of this extraordinary man playing taps, are the words dignity and honor.

Prayer chain for our Military.... Don't break it!

Please send this on after a short prayer. Prayer for our soldiers Don't break it!

Prayer:

'Lord, hold our troops in your loving hands. Protect them as they protect us Bless them and their families for the selfless acts they perform for us in our time of need. Amen.'

Prayer Request: When you receive this, please stop for a moment and say a prayer for our troops around the world.

GOD BLESS YOU FOR PASSING IT ON!

UPDATE! Help A Soldier Through Soldier's Angels!

I have an uncle who is a Vietnam Veteran himself. He just alerted me to an organization that is trying to help soldiers who are still serving in Iraq. The name of the organization is Soldier's Angels. According to my uncle, at present they have 138 soldiers who are awaiting "adoption."

"This organization recruits people to "Adopt a Soldier" to collect items and send packages to one or more of our men. Items included are socks, shaving soap (in tubes no sprays) combs, toothbrushes, sun tan lotion (which are hard to get in Iraq) and the like. Also requested are snacks such as beef jerky, peanuts, etc. or anything that is sealed so that it will not soil," my uncle reported.

To learn more about Soldier's Angels, visit their website at soldiersangels.org.

ATTACK
OF
BUGZILLA
FROM HELL
BY JIM HENRY